Welsh Fairy

Welsh Fairy Tales

Other Stories.

COLLECTED AND EDITED
BY

P. H. EMERSON.

Originally Published By
D. NUTT, 270-271, STRAND.
LONDON
1894

* * * * * * *

Resurrected By
ABELA PUBLISHING
LONDON
2009

Welsh Fairy Tales and Other Stories

Welsh Fairy Tales and Other Stories

Abela Publishing,
London
United Kingdom
2009

ISBN-13: 978-1-907256-03-5

email Books@AbelaPublishing.com

www.AbelaPublishing.com/WelshTales

Dedication

This book is dedicated to the teachers and storytellers

who keep folklore and history alive

through the telling and re-telling

of these tales

Philanthropy

A percentage of the net

from the sale of this book

will be donated towards the education

of underprivileged people in Wales.

Acknowledgements

The Publisher acknowledges the

work that P. H. Emerson did

in compiling this collection of

Welsh Fairy Tales and Other Stories in a time

well before any electronic media was in use.

We also thank those artists who have made

their artwork freely available on the internet.

Art which has made this book decidedly more "Welsh"

in appearance.

AUTHOR'S NOTE.

These tales were collected by me whilst living in Anglesea during the winter 1891-2.

With the exception of the French story, they were told me and I took them down at the time.

Particulars respecting the narratives will be found in the Notes.

In most cases I have done but little "editing", preferring to give the stories as told.

The old book referred to in the Notes I bought from a country bookseller, who knew neither its author, title, or date, but I have since been informed the book is Williams' Observations on the Snowdon Mountains_, published in 1802, a book well known to students of Celtic literature.

P. H. E.

CLARINGBOLD
BROADSTAIRS
April 1894

CONTENTS.

The

Fairies of Paragonan

Once upon a time a lot of fairies lived in Mona.

One day the queen fairy's daughter, who was now fifteen years of age, told her mother she wished to go out and see the world. The queen consented, allowing her to go for a day, and to change from a fairy to a bird, or from a bird to a fairy, as she wished.

When she returned one night she said:
"I've been to a gentleman's house, and as I stood listening, I heard the gentleman was witched: he was very ill, and crying out with pain."

"Oh, I must look into that," said the queen.

So the next day she went through her process and found that he was bewitched by an old witch. So the following day she set out with six other fairies, and when they came to the gentleman's house she found he was very ill.

Going into the room, bearing a small blue pot they had brought with them, the queen asked him:

"Would you like to be cured?"

"Oh, bless you; yes, indeed."

Whereupon the queen put the little blue pot of perfume on the centre of the table, and lit it, when the room was instantly filled with the most delicious odour.

2

Whilst the perfume was burning, the six fairies formed in line behind her, and she leading, they walked round the table three times, chanting in chorus:

> "Round and round three times three,
> We have come to cure thee."

At the end of the third round she touched the burning perfume with her wand, and then touched the gentleman on the head, saying:

"Be thou made whole."

No sooner had she said the words than he jumped up hale and hearty, and said:

"Oh, dear queen, what shall I do for you? I'll do anything you wish."

"Money I do not wish for," said the queen, "but there's a little plot of ground on the sea-cliff I want you to lend me, for I wish to make a ring there, and the grass will die when I make the ring. Then I want you to build three walls round the ring, but leave the sea-side open, so that we may be able to come and go easily."

"With the greatest of pleasure," said the gentleman; and he built the three stone walls at once, at the spot indicated.

3

II.

Near the gentleman lived the old witch, and she had the power of turning at will into a hare. The gentleman was a great hare hunter, but the hounds could never catch this hare; it always disappeared in a mill, running between the wings and jumping in at an open window, though they stationed two men and a dog at the spot, when it immediately turned into the old witch. And the old miller never suspected, for the old woman used to take him a peck of corn to grind a few days before any hunt, telling him she would call for it on the afternoon of the day of the hunt. So that when she arrived she was expected.

One day she had been taunting the gentleman as he returned from a hunt, that he could never catch the hare, and he struck her with his whip, saying "Get away, you witchcraft!"

Whereupon she witched him, and he fell ill, and was cured as we have seen.

When he got well he watched the old witch, and saw she often visited the house of an old miser who lived near by with his beautiful niece. Now all the people in the village touched their hats most respectfully to this old miser, for they knew he had dealings with the witch, and they were as much afraid of him as of her; but everyone loved the miser's kind and beautiful niece.

III.

When the fairies got home the queen told her daughter:

"I have no power over the old witch for twelve months from to-day, and then I have no power over her life. She must lose that by the arm of a man."

So the next day the daughter was sent out again to see whether she could find a person suited to that purpose.

In the village lived a small crofter, who was afraid of nothing; he was the boldest man thereabouts; and one day he passed the miser without saluting him. The old fellow went off at once and told the witch.

"Oh, I'll settle his cows to-night!" said she, and they were taken sick, and gave no milk that night.

The fairy's daughter arrived at his croft-yard after the cows were taken ill, and she heard him say to his son, a bright lad:

"It must be the old witch!"

When she heard this, she sent him to the queen.

So next day the fairy queen took six fairies and went to the croft, taking her blue pot of perfume. When she got there she asked the crofter if he would like his cows cured?

"God bless you, yes!" he said.

The queen made him bring a round table into the yard, whereon she placed the blue pot of perfume, and having lit it, as before, they formed in line and walked round thrice, chanting the words:

> "Round and round three times three,
> We have come to cure thee."

Then she dipped the end of her wand into the perfume, and touched the cows on the forehead, saying to each one:

"Be thou whole."

Whereupon they jumped up cured.

The little farmer was overjoyed, and cried:

"Oh, what can I do for you? What can I do for you?"

"Money I care not for," said the queen, "all I want is your son to avenge you and me."

The lad jumped up and said:

"What I can do I'll do it for you, my lady fairy."

She told him to be at the walled plot the following day at noon, and left.

IV.

The next day at noon, the queen and her daughter and three hundred other fairies came up the cliff to the green grass plot, and they carried a pole, and a tape, and a mirror. When they reached the plot they planted the pole in the ground, and hung the mirror on the pole. The queen took the tape, which measured ten yards and was fastened to the top of the pole, and walked round in a circle, and wherever she set her feet the grass withered and died. Then the fairies followed up behind the queen, and each fairy carried a harebell in her left-hand, and a little blue cup of burning perfume in her right. When they had formed up the queen called the lad to her side, and told him to walk by her throughout. They then started off, all singing in chorus:

> "Round and round three times three,
> Tell me what you see."

When they finished the first round, the queen and lad stopped before the mirror, and she asked the lad what he saw?

> "I see, I see, the mirror tells me,
>   It is the witch that I see,"

said the lad. So they marched round again, singing the same words as before, and when they stopped a second time before the mirror the queen again asked him what he saw?

> "I see, I see, the mirror tells me,
>   It is a hare that I see,"

said the lad.

A third time the ceremony and question were repeated.

> "I see, I see, the mirror tells me,
>   The hares run up the hill to the mill."

"Now", said the queen, "there is to be a hare-hunting this day week; be at the mill at noon, and I will meet you there."

And then the fairies, pole, mirror, and all, vanished and only the empty ring on the green was left.

V.

Upon the appointed day the lad went to his tryst, and at noon the Fairy Queen appeared, and gave him a sling, and a smooth pebble from the beach, saying:

"I have blessed your arms, and I have blessed the sling and the stone.

"Now as the clock strikes three,
Go up the hill near the mill,
And in the ring stand still
Till you hear the click of the mill.
Then with thy arm, with power and might,
You shall strike and smite
The devil of a witch called Jezabel light,
And you shall see an awful sight."

The lad did as he was bidden, and presently he heard the huntsman's horn and the hue and cry, and saw the hare running down the opposite hill-side, where the hounds seemed to gain on her, but as she breasted the hill on which he stood she gained on them. As she came towards the mill he threw his stone, and it lodged in her skull, and when he ran up he found he had killed the old witch. As the huntsmen came up they crowded round him, and praised him; and then they fastened the witch's body to a horse by ropes, and dragged her to the bottom of the valley, where they buried her in a ditch. That night, when the miser heard of her death, he dropped down dead on the spot.

As the lad was going home the queen appeared to him, and told him to be at the ring the following day at noon.

VI.

Next day all the fairies came with the pole and mirror, each carrying a harebell in her left-hand, and a blue cup of burning perfume in her right, and they formed up as before, the lad walking beside the queen. They marched round and repeated the old words, when the queen stopped before the mirror, and said:

"What do you see?"

> "I see, I see, the mirror tells me,
> It is an old plate-cupboard that I see."

A second time they went round, and the question, was repeated.

> "I see, I see, the mirror tells me,
> The back is turned to me."

A third time was the ceremony fulfilled, and the lad answered

> "I see, I see, the mirror tells me,
> A spring-door is open to me."

"Buy that plate-cupboard at the miser's sale," said the queen, and she and her companions disappeared as before.

VII.

Upon the day of the sale all the things were brought out in the road, and the plate-cupboard was put up, the lad recognising it and bidding up for it till it was sold to him. When he had paid for it he took it home in a cart, and when he got in and examined it, he found the secret drawer behind was full of gold. The following week the house and land, thirty acres, was put up for sale, and the lad bought both, and married the miser's niece, and they lived happily till they died.

The

Craig-y-Don Blacksmith

Once upon a time an old blacksmith lived in an old forge at Craig-y-don, and he used to drink a great deal too much beer.

One night he was coming home from an alehouse very tipsy, and as he got near a small stream a lot of little men suddenly sprang up from the rocks, and one of them, who seemed to be older than the rest, came up to him, and said,

"If you don't alter your ways of living you'll die soon; but if you behave better and become a better man you'll find it will be to your benefit," and they all disappeared as quickly as they had come.

The old blacksmith thought a good deal about what the fairies had told him, and he left off drinking, and became a sober, steady man.

One day, a few months after meeting the little people, a strange man brought a horse to be shod. Nobody knew either the horse or the man.

The old blacksmith tied the horse to a hole in the lip of a cauldron (used for the purpose of cooling his hot iron) that he had built in some masonry.

When he had tied the horse up he went to shoe the off hind-leg, but directly he touched the horse the spirited animal started back with a bound, and dragged the cauldron from the masonry, and then it broke the halter and ran away out of the forge, and was never seen again: neither the horse nor its master.

When the old blacksmith came to pull down the masonry to rebuild it, he found three brass kettles full of money.

 Old Gwilym

Old Gwilym Evans started off one fine morning to walk across the Eagle Hills to a distant town, bent upon buying some cheese. On his way, in a lonely part of the hills, he found a golden guinea, which he quickly put into his pocket.

When he got to the town, instead of buying his provisions, he went into an alehouse, and sat drinking and singing with some sweet-voiced quarrymen until dark, when he thought it was time to go home. Whilst he was drinking, an old woman with a basket came in, and sat beside him, but she left before him. After the parting glass he got up and reeled through the town, quite forgetting to buy his cheese; and as he got amongst the hills they seemed to dance up and down before him, and he seemed to be walking on air. When he got near the lonely spot where he had found the money he heard some sweet music, and a number of fairies crossed his path and began dancing all round him, and then as he looked up he saw some brightly-lighted houses before him on the hill; and he scratched his head, for he never remembered having seen houses thereabouts before. And as he was thinking, and watching the fairies, one came and begged him to come into the house and sit down.

So he followed her in, and found the house was all gold inside it, and brightly lighted, and the fairies were dancing and singing, and they brought him anything he wanted for supper, and then they put him to bed.

Gwilym slept heavily, and when he awoke turned round, for he felt very cold, and his body seemed covered with prickles; so he sat up and rubbed his eyes, and found that he was quite naked and lying in a bunch of gorse.

When he found himself in this plight he hurried home, and told his wife, and she was very angry with him for spending all the money and bringing no cheese home, and then he told her his adventures.

"Oh, you bad man!" she said, "the fairies gave you money and you spent it wrongly, so they were sure to take their revenge."

The Baby-Farmer

Old Kaddy was a baby-farmer, and one day she went to the woods to gather sticks for her fire, and whilst she was gathering the sticks she found a piece of gold, and took it home; but she never told anyone she had found the money, for she always pretended to be very poor.

But though she was so poor, she used to dress two of her children in fine clothes; but the others, whom she did not like, she kept in the filthiest rags.

One day a man knocked at her door, and asked to see the children.

He sat down in her little room, and she went and brought the ragged little boy and girl, saying she was very poor, and couldn't afford to dress them better; for she had been careful to hide the well-dressed little boy and girl in a cockloft.

After the stranger had gone she went to the cockloft to look for her well-dressed favourites, but they had disappeared, and they were never seen afterwards, for they were turned into fairies.

The Old Man and the Fairies

Many years ago the Welsh mountains were full of fairies. People used to go by moonlight to see them dancing, for they knew where they would dance by seeing green rings in the grass.

There was an old man living in those days who used to frequent the fairs that were held across the mountains. One day he was crossing the mountains to a fair, and when he got to a lonely valley he sat down, for he was tired, and he dropped off to sleep, and his bag fell down by his side. When he was sound asleep the fairies came and carried him off, bag and all, and took him under the earth, and when he awoke he found himself in a great palace of gold, full of fairies dancing and singing. And they took him and showed him everything, the splendid gold room and gardens, and they kept dancing round him until he fell asleep.

When he was asleep they carried him back to the same spot where they had found him, and when he awoke he thought he had been dreaming, so he looked for his bag, and got hold of it, but he could hardly lift it. When he opened it he found it was nearly filled with gold.

He managed to pick it up, and turning round, he went home.

When he got home, his wife Kaddy said: "What's to do, why haven't you been to the fair?" "I've got something here," he said, and showed his wife the gold.

"Why, where did you get that?"

But he wouldn't tell her. Since she was curious, like all women, she kept worrying him all night--for he'd put the money in a box under the bed--so he told her about the fairies.

Next morning, when he awoke, he thought he'd go to the fair and buy a lot of things, and he went to the box to get some of the gold, but found it full of cockle-shells.

Tommy Pritchard

Tommy Pritchard was going to school one day, and on his way he thought he heard somebody singing on the other side of a stone wall by the road, so he climbed up and looked over, and there underneath a stone he saw a sixpence, so he took it.

Every morning after that, when he went to school, he used to look in the same place, and he always found a sixpence.

His father noticed he was always spending money in the sweet-shop, so he began to think Tommy was stealing from somebody, and one day he asked him where he got the money. Tommy wouldn't tell at first, but his father threatened to beat him, so he told him where he got his sixpences.

Next morning he went to look in the same place for his sixpence, and he found nothing but a cockle-shell. And he never saw anything but a cockle-shell there afterwards.

 Maddy's Luck

There was a tall young woman whom the fairies used to visit, coming through the keyhole at night. She could hear them dancing and singing in her room, but in the morning they used to go the way they had come, only they always left her some money.

When she got married she chose a tall husband like herself, and they had a fine big child.

One night they went to a fair, and they got to one side to hear the fairies; for some people could tell when the fairies were coming, for they made a noise like the wind. Whilst they were waiting she told her husband how the fairies used to leave her money at night.

When they got home they found their baby all right, and went to bed. But next morning the young mother found her child had been changed in the night, and there was a very little baby in the cradle. And the child never grew big, for the fairies had changed her child for spite.

The  Story of Gelert
(As current in Anglesea)

It was somewhere about 1200, Prince Llewellyn had a castle at Aber, just abreast of us here; indeed, parts of the towers remain to this day. His consort was the Princess Joan; she was King John's daughter. Her coffin remains with us to this day. Llewellyn was a great hunter of wolves and foxes, for the hills of Carnarvonshire were infested with wolves in those days, after the young lambs.

Now the prince had several hunting-houses--sorts of farm houses, one of them was at the place now called Beth-Gelert, for the wolves were very thick there at this time. Now the prince used to travel from farm-house to farm-house with his family and friends, when going on these hunting parties.

One season they went hunting from Aber, and stopped at the house where Beth-Gelert is now--it's about fourteen miles away. The prince had all his hounds with him, but his favourite was Gelert, a hound who had never let off a wolf for six years.

The prince loved the dog like a child, and at the sound of his horn Gelert was always the first to come bounding up. There was company at the house, and one day they went hunting, leaving his wife and the child, in a big wooden cradle, behind him at the farm-house.

The hunting party killed three or four wolves, and about two hours before the word passed for returning home, Llewellyn missed Gelert, and he asked his huntsmen:

"Where's Gelert? I don't see him."

"Well, indeed, master, I've missed him this half-hour."

And Llewellyn blew his horn, but no Gelert came at the sound.

Indeed, Gelert had got on to a wolves' track which led to the house.

The prince sounded the return, and they went home, the prince lamenting Gelert. "He's sure to have been slain--he's sure to have been slain! since he did not answer the horn. Oh, my Gelert!" And they approached the house, and the prince went into the house, and saw Gelert lying by the overturned cradle, and blood all about the room.

"What! hast thou slain my child?" said the prince, and ran his sword through the dog.

After that he lifted up the cradle to look for his child, and found the body of a big wolf underneath that Gelert had slain, and his child was safe. Gelert had capsized the cradle in the scuffle.

"Oh, Gelert! Oh, Gelert!" said the prince, "my favourite hound, my favourite hound! Thou hast been slain by thy master's hand, and in death thou hast licked thy master's hand!" He patted the dog, but it was too late, and poor Gelert died licking his master's hand.

Next day they made a coffin, and had a regular funeral, the same as if it were a human being; all the servants in deep mourning, and everybody. They made him a grave, and the village was called after the dog, Beth-Gelert--Gelert's Grave; and the prince planted a tree, and put a gravestone of slate, though it was before the days of quarries. And they are to be seen to this day.

Origin of the Welsh

Many years ago there lived several wild tribes round the King of Persia's city, and the king's men were always annoying and harassing them, exacting yearly a heavy tribute. Now these tribes, though very brave in warfare, could not hold their own before the Persian army when sent out against them, so that they paid their yearly tribute grudgingly, but took revenge, whenever they could, upon travellers to or from the city, robbing and killing them.

At last one of the tribesmen, a clever old chieftain, thought of a cunning plan whereby to defeat the Persians, and free themselves from the yearly tribute. And this was his scheme:

The wild wastes where these tribes lived were infested with large birds called "Rohs"[1], which were very destructive to human beings--devouring men, women, and children greedily whenever they could catch them. Such a terror were they that the tribes had to protect their village with high walls[2], and then they slept securely, for the Roh hunted by night. This old chieftain determined to watch the birds, and find out their nesting-places; so he had a series of towers built, in which the watchmen could sleep securely by night. These towers were advanced in whatever direction the birds were seen to congregate by night. The observers reported that the Roh could not fly, but ran very swiftly, being fleeter than any horse.

At length, by watching, their nesting-places were found in a sandy plain, and it was discovered that those monstrous birds stole sheep and cattle in great numbers.

---

[1] Pronounced softly.
[2] Can this have anything to do with the idea of walling-in the cuckoo?

The chieftain then gave orders for the watchmen to keep on guard until the young birds were hatched, when they were commanded to secure fifty, and bring them into the walled town. The order was carried out, and one night they secured fifty young birds just out of the egg, and brought them to the town.

The old chieftain then told off fifty skilful warriors, a man to each bird, to his son being allotted the largest bird. These warriors were ordered to feed the birds on flesh, and to train them for battle. The birds grew up as tame as horses. Saddles and bridles were made for them, and they were trained and exercised just like chargers.

When the next tribute day came round, the King of Persia sent his emissaries to collect the tax, but the chieftains of the tribes insulted and defied them, so that they returned to the king, who at once sent forward his army.

The chieftain then marshalled his men, and forty-six of the Rohs were drawn up in front of the army, the chief getting on the strongest bird. The remaining four were placed on the right flank, and ordered at a signal to advance and cut off the army, should they retreat.

The Rohs had small scales, like those of a fish, on their necks and bodies, the scales being hidden under a soft hair, except on the upper half of the neck. They had no feathers except on their wings. So they were invulnerable except as to the eyes--for in those days the Persians only had bows and arrows, and light javelins. When the Persian army advanced, the Rohs advanced at lightning speed, and made fearful havoc, the birds murdering and trampling the soldiers under foot, and beating them down with their powerful wings. In less than two hours half the

Persian army was slain, and the rest had escaped. The tribes returned to their walled towns, delighted with their victory.

When the news of his defeat reached the King of Persia he was wroth beyond expression, and could not sleep for rage. So the next morning he called for his magician.

"What are you going to do with the birds?" asked the king.

"Well, I've been thinking the matter over," replied the magician.

"Cannot you destroy all of them?"

"No, your majesty; I cannot destroy them, for I have not the power; but I can get rid of them in one way; for though I cannot put out life, I have the power of turning one life into some other living creature."

"Well, what will you turn them into?" asked the king.

"I'll consider to-night, your majesty," replied the magician.

"Well, mind and be sure to do it."

"Yes, I'll be sure to do it, your majesty."

*   *   *   *   *

The next day, at ten, the magician appeared before the king, who asked:

"Have you considered well?"

"Yes, your majesty."

"Well, how are you going to act?"

26

"Your majesty, I've thought and thought during the night, and the best thing we can do is to turn all the birds into fairies."

"What are fairies?" asked the king.

"I've planned it all out, and I hope your majesty will agree."

"Oh! I'll agree, as long as they never molest us more."

"Well, your majesty, I'm going to turn them to fairies--small living creatures to live in caves in the bowels of the earth, and they shall only visit people living on the earth once a year. They shall be harmless, and hurt nothing; they shall be fairies, and do nothing but dance and sing, and I shall allow them to go about on earth for twenty-four hours once a year and play their antics, but they shall do no mischief."

"How long are the birds to remain in that state?" asked the king.

"I'll give them 2,000 years, your majesty; and at the end of that time they are to go back into birds, as they were before. And after the birds change from the fairy state back into birds, they shall never breed more, but die a natural death."

So the tribes lost their birds, and the King of Persia made such fearful havoc amongst them that they decided to leave the country.

They travelled, supporting themselves by robbery; until they came to a place where they built a city, and called it Troy, where they were besieged for a long time.

At length the besiegers built a large caravan, with a large man's head in front; the head was all gilded with gold. When the caravan was finished they put 150 of the best warriors inside, provided with food, and one of them had a trumpet. Then they pulled the caravan, which ran upon eight broad wheels, up to the gates of the city, and left it there, their army being drawn up in a valley near by. It was, agreed that when the caravan got inside the gates the bugler should blow three loud blasts to warn, the army, who would immediately advance into the city.

The men on the ramparts saw this curious caravan, and they began wondering what it was, and for two or three days they left it alone.

At last an old chieftain said, "It must be their food."

On the third day they opened the gates, and attaching ropes, began to haul it into the city; then the warriors leaped out, and the horn blew, and the army hurried up, and the town was taken after great slaughter; but a number escaped with their wives and children, and fled on to the Crimea, whence they were driven by the Russians, so they marched away along the sea to Spain, and bearing up through France, they stopped. Some wanted to go across the sea, and some stayed in the heart of France: they were the Bretoons[1]. The others came on over in boats, and landed in England, and they were the first people settled in Great Britain: they were the Welsh.

---

[1] Bretons

ROWS

One black crow, bad luck for me.
Two black crows, good luck for me.
Three black crows, a son shall be born in the family.
Four black crows, a daughter shall be born in the family.
Five black crows shall be a funeral in the family.
Six black crows, if they fly head on, a sudden death.
Seven black crows with their tails towards you,
    death within seven years.

There was a young man, not so very long ago, who had been to sea for years. He was married, but had no children. He was one of the most spirited men you ever saw. He used to complain of his dreams. He said, "All at once last Sunday I was up in the air, and I saw the vessel I was in going at great speed, making for a mountain, and I tried as hard as I could to keep her from the mountain. I don't believe I was asleep at all, I could see it so plainly. I went along in the air, looking at seven black crows all the time. I got dizzy, and the vessel seemed to lower on to the earth. The vessel lowered within a few hundred feet of the earth, and I saw what I thought were fairies. I thought I had been there for days; in truth, it seemed to me I had been up there for three days, and that I could hear the fairies with mournful sounds drawing a coffin. I watched and watched, and saw seven crows on the coffin. It seemed as if they were going to bury someone. Whilst the coffin was going the seven crows flew up and bursted, and the heavens were illuminated more strongly than by the sun. Then I lost sight of the fairies, but saw some big giants in white walking about, and there was a big throne with a roof to it. And all at once I was in total darkness, but I could hear things flapping about, flying through the air. Then I saw the moon rising and all the stars, and all sorts of objects flying through the air. And one came to me, and put his hand

30

upon my shoulder, saying: _'Prepare to meet us to-morrow.'_
After that everything went dark again. The first thing I knew I
was in a ship steering, and the seven black crows were in front
of me. I had a great trouble to steer my vessel. And as I went on
the vessel struck a steeple, and exploded, and I awoke.
Whereupon I jumped out of bed, looking very pale."

I left him on the beach at 11.30, after he told me this, when he
went home. When he got home he could see seven black crows
on the house. Other people could see the crows, but could not
count them. He saw them all perched head on. He went into the
house, and said,

"There is something in these crows, Jane; see them on the roof."

She cried out and ran out and looked, but could not see the
seven. After that he didn't seem to be himself, though there was
nothing the matter with him. A week afterwards, I went out on
the Sunday morning after breakfast, and there was a seat on the
beach, and on it sat this man, Johnny, and another man.

"Why, Johnny, you look very pale," I said.
"Do I?" he said.
"Yes! indeed you do," I replied.
"Well, I don't know, I have had such dreams."
"What will they have been, then?" I asked.
"That I was in a full-rigged ship, with all sails set; I was all
alone, but could see nothing, only seven black crows. I counted
them, but my wife could see nothing, but she could hear
something."

That same day, when he went home, he said to his wife:
"Ah, Jane, there is something coming over me," and he fell down
dead.

 Robert Roberts and the Fairies

Robert Roberts was a carpenter who worked hard and well; but he could never keep his tongue still. One day, as he was crossing a brook, a little man came up to him and said:

"Robert Roberts, go up to the holly tree that leans over the road on the Red-hill, and dig below it, and you shall be rewarded."

The very next morning, at daybreak, Robert Roberts set out for the spot, and dug a great hole, before anyone was up, when he found a box of gold. He went to the same place twice afterwards, and dug, and found gold each time. But as he grew rich, he began to boast and hint that he had mysterious friends. One day, when the talk turned on the fairies, he said that he knew them right well, and that they gave him money. Robert Roberts thought no more of the matter until he went to the spot a week afterwards, one evening at dusk. When he got to the tree, and began to dig as usual, big stones came rolling down the bank, just missing him, so that he ran for his life, and never went near the place again.

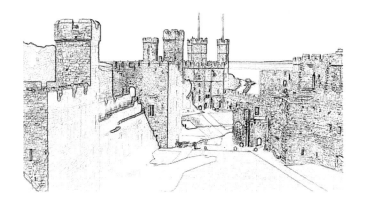

The Fairy of the Dell

In olden times fairies were sent to oppose the evil-doings of witches, and to destroy their power. About three hundred years ago a band of fairies, sixty in number, with their queen, called Queen of the Dell, came to Mona to oppose the evil works of a celebrated witch. The fairies settled by a spring, in a valley. After having blessed the spring, or "well", as they called it, they built a bower just above the spring for the queen, placing a throne therein. Near by they built a large bower for themselves to live in.

After that, the queen drew three circles, one within the other, on a nice flat grassy place by the well. When they were comfortably settled, the queen sent the fairies about the country to gather tidings of the people. They went from house to house, and everywhere heard great complaints against an old witch; how she had made some blind, others lame, and deformed others by causing a horn to grow out of their foreheads. When they got back to the well and told the queen, she said:

"I must do something for these old people, and though the witch is very powerful, we must break her power." So the next day the queen fairy sent word to all the bewitched to congregate upon a fixed day at the sacred well, just before noon.

When the day came, several ailing people collected at the well. The queen then placed the patients in pairs in the inner ring, and the sixty fairies in pairs in the middle ring. Each little fairy was three feet and a half high, and carried a small wand in her right hand, and a bunch of fairy flowers--cuckoo's boots, baby's bells, and day's-eyes--in her left hand. Then the queen, who was four feet and a half in height, took the outside ring. On her head was a crown of wild flowers, in her right hand she carried a wand,

34

and in her left a posy of fairy flowers. At a signal from the queen they began marching round the rings, singing in chorus:

"We march round by two and two
The circles of the sacred well
That lies in the dell."

When they had walked twice round the ring singing, the queen took her seat upon the throne, and calling each patient to her, she touched him with her wand and bade him go down to the sacred well and dip his body into the water three times, promising that all his ills should be cured. As each one came forth from the spring he knelt before the queen, and she blessed him, and told him to hurry home and put on dry clothes. So that all were cured of their ills.

II.

Now the old witch who had worked all these evils lived near the well in a cottage. She had first learned witchcraft from a book called "The Black Art", which a gentleman farmer had lent her when a girl. She progressed rapidly with her studies, and being eager to learn more, sold herself to the devil, who made compact with her that she should have full power for seven years, after which she was to become his. He gave her a wand that had the magic power of drawing people to her, and she had a ring on the grass by her house just like the fairy's ring. As the seven years were drawing to a close, and her heart was savage against the farmer who first led her into the paths of evil knowledge, she determined to be revenged. One day, soon after the Fairy of the Dell came to live by the spring, she drew the farmer to her with her wand, and, standing in her ring, she lured him into it. When he crossed the line, she said:

"Cursed be he or she
That crosses my circle to see me,"

and, touching him on the head and back, a horn and a tail grew from the spots touched. He went off in a terrible rage, but she only laughed maliciously. Then, as she heard of the Queen of the Dell's good deeds, she repented of her evil deeds, and begged her neighbour to go to the queen fairy and ask her if she might come and visit her. The queen consented, and the old witch went down and told her everything--of the book, of the magic wand, of the ring, and of all the wicked deeds she had done.

"O, you have been a bad witch," said the queen, "but I will see what I can do; but you must bring me the book and the wand;" and she told the old witch to come on the following day a little before noon. When the witch came the next day with her wand and book, she found the fairies had built a fire in the middle ring. The queen then took her and stood her by the fire, for she could not trust her on the outer circle.

"Now I must have more power," said the queen to the fairies, and she went and sat on the throne, leaving the witch by the fire in the middle ring. After thinking a little, the queen said, "Now I have it," and coming down from her throne muttering, she began walking round the outer circle, waiting for the hour of one o'clock, when all the fairies got into the middle circle and marched round, singing:

> "At the hour of one
> The cock shall crow one,
> Goo! Goo! Goo!
> I am here to tell
> Of the sacred well
> That lies in the dell,
> And will conquer hell."

On the second round, they sang:
> "At the hour of two
> The cock crows two,
> Goo! Goo! Goo!
> I am here to tell
> Of the sacred well
> That lies in the dell;
> We will conquer hell."

At the last round, they sang:
> "At the hour of three
> The cock crows three,
> Goo! Goo! Goo!
> I am here to tell
> Of the sacred well
> That lies in the dell;
> Now I have conquered hell."

Then the queen cast the book and wand into the fire, and immediately the vale was rent by a thundering noise, and numbers of devils came from everywhere, and encircled the outer ring, but they could not pass the ring. Then the fairies began walking round and round, singing their song. When they had finished the song they heard a loud screech from the devils that frightened all the fairies except the queen. She was unmoved, and going to the fire, stirred the ashes with her wand, and saw that the book and wand were burnt, and then she walked thrice round the outer ring by herself, when she turned to the devils, and said:

"I command you to be gone from our earthly home, get to your own abode. I take the power of casting you all from here. Begone! begone! begone!" And all the devils flew up, and there was a mighty clap as of thunder, and the earth trembled, and the sky became overcast, and all the devils burst, and the sky cleared again.

After this the queen put three fairies by the old witch's side, and they constantly dipped their wands in the sacred spring, and touched her head, and she was sorely troubled and converted.

"Bring the mirror," said the queen.

And the fairies brought the mirror and laid it in the middle circle, and they all walked round three times, chanting again the song beginning "At the hour of one." When they had done this the queen stood still, and said:

"Stand and watch to see what you can see."

And as she looked she said:

> "The mirror shines unto me
> That the witch we can see
> Has three devils inside of she."

Immediately the witch had a fit, and the three fairies had a hard job to keep the three devils quiet; indeed, they could not do so, and the queen had to go herself with her wand, for fear the devils should burst the witch asunder, and she said, "Come out three evil spirits, out of thee."

And they came gnashing their teeth, and would have killed all the fairies, but the queen said:

"Begone, begone, begone! you evil spirits, to the place of your abode," and suddenly the sky turned bright as fire, for the evil spirits were trying their spleen against the fairies, but the queen said, "Collect, collect, collect, into one fierce ball," and the fiery sky collected into one ball of fire more dazzling than the sun, so that none could look at it except the queen, who wore a black silk mask to protect her eyes. Suddenly the ball burst with a terrific noise, and the earth trembled.

"Enter into your abode, and never come down to our abode on earth any more," said the queen.

And the witch was herself again, and she and the queen fairy were immediately great friends. The witch, when she came out of the ring, dropped on her knee and asked the queen if she might call her the Lady of the Dell, and how she could serve her.

"We will see about that," said the queen.

"Well, how do you live?" asked the woman who had been a witch.

"Well, I'll tell you," said the queen. "We go at midnight and milk the cows, and we keep the milk, and it never grows less so long as we leave some in the bottom of the vessel; we must not use it all. After milking the cow, we rub the cow's purse and bless it, and she gives double the amount of milk."

"Well, how do you get corn?"

"Well, we were at the mill playing one day, and the miller came in and saw us, and spoke kindly to us, and offered us some flour. 'We never take nothing for nothing,' I said, so I blessed the bin: so in a few minutes the bin was full to the brim with flour, and I said to the miller, 'Now don't you empty the bin, but always leave a peck in it, and for twelve months, no matter how much you use the bin, it will always be full in the morning.' Now I have told you this much, and I will tell further, 'You must love your neighbour, you must love all mankind.' Now here is a purse of gold, go and buy what you want, eggs, bacon, cheese, and get a flagon of wine and use these things freely, giving freely to the aged poor, and if you never finish these things,

there will always be as much the next morning as you started
with. And I shall make a salve for you, and you must use the
water from the sacred well. That will be as a medicine, and
people shall come from far and wide to be cured by you, and
you shall be loved by all, and you shall be known to the poorest
of the poor as Madame Dorothy."

And the woman did as she was told, and she became renowned
for her medical skill, especially in childbirth, for her salve eased
the pains, and her waters brought milk. By-and-by, she got
known all over the island, and rich people came to her from
afar, and she always made the rich pay, and the poor were
treated free.

Madame Dorothy used to see the queen fairy at times, and one
day she asked her, "Shall we meet again?"

"We cannot tell," said the queen, "but I will give you a ring--let
me place it on your finger--it is a magic ring worked by fairies.
Whenever you seek to know of me, make a ring of your own,
and walk round three times and rub the ring; if it turns bright I
am alive, but if you see blood I am dead."

"But how can that be? You are much younger than I am."

"Oh, no! we fairies look young to the day of our death; we live to
a great age, but die naturally of old age, for we never have any
ailments, but still our power fades. Men fade in the flesh and
power, but we fade only in power. I am over seventy now."

"But you look to be thirty."

"Well, we will shake hands and part, for I must go elsewhere; as
I have no king, I do not stop in one place."

And they shook hands and parted.

Ellen's Luck

Ellen was a good girl, and beautiful to look upon. One Sunday she was walking by an open gutter in a town in North Wales when she found a copper. After that day Ellen walked every Sunday afternoon by the same drain, and always found a copper. She was a careful girl, and used to hoard her money.

One day her old mother found her pile of pennies, and wished to know where she got them.

Ellen told her, but though she walked by the gutter for many a Sunday after, she never found another copper.

The Fairies' Mint

Once upon a time there was a miller, who lived in Anglesey. One day he noticed that some of his sacks had been moved during the night. The following day he felt sure that some of his grain had been disturbed, and, lastly, he was sure someone had been working his mill in the night during his absence. He confided his suspicions to a friend, and they determined to go the next night and watch the mill. The following night, at about midnight, as they approached the mill, that stood on a bare stony hill, they were surprised to find the mill all lit up and at work, the great sails turning in the black night. Creeping up softly to a small window, the miller looked in, and saw a crowd of little men carrying small bags, and emptying them into the millstones. He could not see, however, what was in the bags, so he crept to another window, when he saw golden coins coming from the mill, from the place where the flour usually ran out.

Immediately the miller went to the mill door, and, putting his key into the lock, he unlocked the door; and as he did so the lights went out suddenly, and the mill stopped working. As he and his friend went into the dark mill they could hear sounds of people running about, but by the time they lit up the mill again there was nobody to be seen, but scattered all about the millstones and on the floor were cockle-shells.

After that, many persons who passed the mill at midnight said they saw the mill lit up and working; but the old miller left the fairies alone to coin their money.

The Bellings

In a meadow belonging to Ystrad, bounded by the river which falls from Cwellyn Lake, they say the fairies used to assemble, and dance in fair moonlight nights. One evening a young man, who was the heir and occupier of this farm, hid himself in a thicket close to the spot where they used to gambol. Presently they appeared, and when in their merry mood, out he bounced from his covert, and seized one of their females; the rest of the company dispersed themselves, and disappeared in an instant. Disregarding her struggles and screams, he hauled her to his home, where he treated her so very kindly that she became contented to live with him as his maid-servant, but he could not prevail upon her to tell him her name. Some time after, happening again to see the fairies upon the same spot, he heard one of them saying, "The last time we met here our sister Penelope was snatched away from us by one of the mortals." Rejoiced at knowing the name of his incognita, he returned home; and as she was very beautiful and extremely active, he proposed to marry her, which she would not for a long time consent to; at last, however, she complied, but on this condition, "That if ever he should strike her with iron, she would leave him, and never return to him again." They lived happy for many years together, and he had by her a son and a daughter; and by her industry and prudent management as a housewife he became one of the richest men in the country. He farmed, besides his own freehold, all the lands on the north side of Nant y Bettws to the top of Snowdon, and all Cwm brwynog in Llanberis, an extent of about five thousand acres or upwards.

Unfortunately, one day Penelope followed her husband into the field to catch a horse, and he, being in a rage at the animal as he ran away from him, threw at him the bridle that was in his hand, which unluckily fell on poor Penelope. She disappeared in an instant, and he never saw her afterwards, but heard her voice in the window of his room one night after, requesting him to take care of the children, in these words:--

> "Rhag bod anwyd ar fy mab,
>   Yn rhodd rhowch arno gob ei dad:
>   Rhag bod anwyd ar liw'r cann,
>   Rhoddwch arni bais ei mam."

That is,

> "Oh! lest my son should suffer cold,
>   Him in his father's coat infold:
>   Lest cold should seize my darling fair,
>   For her, her mother's robe prepare."

These children and their descendants they say were called Pellings[1], a word corrupted from their mother's name Penelope.

* * * * * *

[1] *In England we frequently meet with the surname Pilling and Billing; it might have happened, that a man had met with an English woman of that name, and had married her, and, as is usual in brides, she might have been, though married, called by her maiden name, and the appellation might have been continued to her posterity.--*
Authors Note.

The name Billing and Belling is the family name of one of the oldest Cornish (Keltic) families--a fact that suggests other possibilities.
--P. H. E.

The ong-ived ncestors

The Eagle of Gwernabwy had been long married to his female, and had by her many children; she died, and he continued a long time a widower; but at length be proposed a marriage with the Owl of Cwm Cwmlwyd; but afraid of her being young, so as to have children by her, and thereby degrade his own family, he first of all went to inquire about her age amongst the aged of the world. Accordingly he applied to the Stag of Rhedynfre, whom he found lying close to the trunk of an old oak, and requested to know the Owl's age.

"I have seen," said the Stag, "this oak an acorn, which is now fallen to the ground through age, without either bark or leaves, and never suffered any hurt or strain except from my rubbing myself against it once a day, after getting up on my legs; but I never remember to have seen the Owl you mention younger or older than she seems to be at this day. But there is one older than I am, and that is the Salmon of Glynllifon."

The Eagle then applied to the Salmon for the age of the Owl. The Salmon answered, "I am as many years old as there are scales upon my skin, and particles of spawn within my belly; yet never saw I the Owl you mention but the same in appearance. But there is one older than I am, and that is the Blackbird of Cilgwri."

The Eagle next repaired to the Blackbird of Cilgwri, whom he found perched upon a small stone, and enquired of him the Owl's age.

48

"Dost thou see this stone upon which I sit," said the Blackbird, "which is now no bigger than what a man can carry in his hand? I have seen this very stone of such weight as to be a sufficient load for a hundred oxen to draw, which has suffered neither rubbing nor wearing, save that I rub my bill on it once every evening, and touch the tips of my wings on it every morning, when I expand them to fly; yet I have not seen the Owl either older or younger than she appears to be at this day. But there is one older than I am, and that is the Frog of Mochno Bog, and if he does not know her age, there is not a creature living that does know it."

The Eagle went last of all to the Frog and desired to know the Owl's age. He answered, "I never ate anything but the dust from the spot which I inhabit, and that very sparingly, and dost thou see these great hills that surround and overawe this bog where I lie? They are formed only of the excrements from my body since I have inhabited this place, yet I never remember to have seen the Owl but an old hag, making that hideous noise, Too, hoo, hoo! always frightening the children in the neighbourhood."

So the Eagle of Gwernabwy, the Stag of Rhedynfre, the Salmon of Glynllifon, the Blackbird of Cilgwri, the Frog of Mochno Bog, and the Owl of Cwm Cawlwyd are the oldest creatures in the whole world!

The Giantess's Apron-Full

A huge giant, in company with his wife, travelling towards the island of Mona, with an intention of settling amongst the first inhabitants that had removed there, and having been informed that there was but a narrow channel which divided it from the continent, took up two large stones, one under each arm, to carry with him as a preparatory for making a bridge over this channel, and his lady had her apron filled with small stones for the same purpose; but, meeting a man on this spot with a large parcel of old shoes on his shoulders, the giant asked him how far it was to Mona. The man replied, that it was so far, that he had worn out those shoes in travelling from Mona to that place. The giant on hearing this dropped down the stones, one on each side of him, where they now stand upright, about a hundred yards or more distant from each other; the space between them was occupied by this Goliah's body. His mistress at the same time opened her apron, and dropped down the contents of it, which formed this heap.

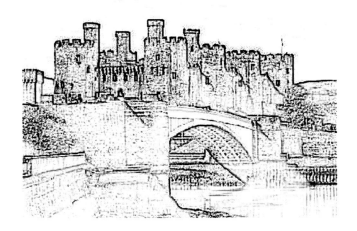

Gwrgan Barforwch's Fable

Hear me, O ye Britons! On the top of a high rock in Arvon there stood a goat, which a lion perceiving from the valley below, addressed her in this manner:--

"My dearest neighbour, why preferrest thou that dry barren rock to feed on? Come down to this charming valley, where thou mayest feed luxuriously upon all sorts of dainties, amongst flowers in shady groves, made fruitful by meandering brooks."

"I am much obliged to you, master," replied the goat; "perhaps you mean well, and tell me the truth, but you have very bad neighbours, whom I do not like to trust, and those are your teeth, so, with your leave, I prefer staying where I am."

The Story of the Pig-Trough

In the beginning of the century, Hughes went as military substitute for a farmer's son. He got L80, a watch, and a suit of clothes. His mother was loath to let him go, and when he joined his regiment, she followed him from Amlych to Pwlheli to try and buy him off. He would not hear of it. "Mother," he said, "the whole of Anglesey would not keep me, I want to be off, and see the world."

The regiment was quartered in Edinboro', and Hughes married the daughter of the burgess with whom he was billeted. Thence, leaving a small son, as hostage to the grandparents, they went to Ireland, and Hughes and his wife were billeted on a pork-butcher's family in Dublin. One day, the mother of the pork-butcher, an old granny, told them she had seen the fairies.

"Last night, as I was abed, I saw a bright, bright light come in, and afterwards a troop of little angels. They danced all over my bed, and they played and sang music--oh! the sweetest music ever I heard. I lay and watched them and listened. By-and-bye the light went out and the music stopped, and I saw them no more. I regretted the music very much. But directly after another smaller light appeared, and a tall dark man came up to my bed, and with something in his hand he tapped me on the temple; it felt like some one drawing a sharp pin across my temple then he went too. In the morning my pillow was covered with blood. I thought and thought, and then I knew I had moved the pig's trough and must have put it in the fairies' path and the fairies were angered, and the king of the fairies had punished me for it." She moved the trough back to its old place the next day, and received no more visits from the wee folk.

Billy Duffy

and the Devil

Billy Duffy was an Irishman, a blacksmith, and a drunkard. He had the Keltic aversion from steady work, and stuck to his forge only long enough to get money for drink; when that was spent, he returned to work.

Billy was coming home one day after one of these drinking-bouts, soberer than usual, when he exclaimed to himself, for the thirst was upon him, "By God! I would sell myself to the devil if I could get some more drink."

At that moment a tall gentleman in black stepped up to him, and said, "What did you say?"

"I said I would sell myself to the devil if I could get a drink."

"Well, how much do you want for seven years, and the devil to get you then?"

"Well, I can't tell exactly, when it comes to the push."

"Will £700 do you?"

"Yes; I'd take £700."

"And the devil to get you then?"

"Oh, yes; I don't care about that."

When Billy got home he found the money in his smithy. He at once shut the smithy, and began squandering the money, keeping open house.

Amongst the people who flocked to get what they could out of Billy came an old hermit, who said, "I am very hungry, and nearly starved.
Will you give me something to eat and drink?"

"Oh, yes; come in and get what you like."

The hermit disappeared, after eating and drinking, and did not reappear for several months, when he received the same kindly welcome, again disappearing. A few months afterwards he again appeared.

"Come in, come in!" said Billy.

After he had eaten and drunk his full, the hermit said to Billy: "Well, three times have you been good and kind to me. I'll give you three wishes, and whatever you wish will be sure to come true."

"I must have time to consider," said Billy.

"Oh, you shall have plenty of time to consider, and mind they are good wishes."

Next morning Billy told the hermit he was ready. "Well, go on; be sure they're good wishes," said the hermit.

"Well, I've got a big sledge-hammer in the smithy, and I wish whoever gets hold of that hammer shall go on striking the anvil, and never break it, till I tell him to stop."

"Oh, that's a bad wish, Billy."

"Oh, no; you'll see it's good. Next thing I wish for is a purse so that no one can take out whatever I put into it."

"Oh, Billy, Billy! that's a bad wish. Be careful now about the third wish," said the hermit.

"Well, I have got an armchair upstairs, and I wish that whoever may sit in that armchair will never be able to get up till I let them."

"Well, well, indeed; they are not very good wishes."

"Oh, yes; I've got my senses about me. I think I'll make them good wishes, after all."

The seven years, all but three days, had passed, and Billy was back working at his forge, for all his money was gone, when the dark gentleman stepped in and said:

"Now, Billy, during these last three days you may have as much money as you like," and he disappeared.

On the last day of his seven years Billy was penniless, and he went to the taproom of his favourite inn, which was full.

"Well, boys," said Billy, "we must have some money to-night. I'll treat you, and give you a pound each," and rising, he placed his tumbler in the middle of the table, and wished for twenty pounds. No sooner had he wished than a ball of fire came through the ceiling, and the twenty sovereigns fell into the tumbler. Everyone was taken aback, and there was a noise as if a bomb had burst, and the fireball disappeared, and rolled down the garden path, the landlord following it. After this they each drank what they liked, and Billy gave them a sovereign apiece before he went home.

The next morning he was in his smithy making a pair of horseshoes, when the devil came in and said:

"Well, Billy, I'll want you this morning."

"Yes; all right. Take hold of this sledge-hammer, and give me a few hammers till I finish this job before I go."

So the devil seized the hammer and began striking the anvil, but he couldn't stop.

So Billy laughed, and locked him in, and was away three days. During this time the people collected round the smithy, and peeped through the cracks in the shutter, for they could hear the hammer going night and day.

At the end of three days Billy returned and opened the door, and the devil said, "Oh, Billy, you've played a fine trick to me; let me go."

"What are you going to give me if I let you go?"

"Seven years more, twice the money, and two days' grace for wishing for what you like."

The devil paid his money and disappeared, and Billy shut the smithy and took to gambling and drinking, so that at the end of seven years he was without a penny, and working again in his smithy.

On the last night of the seven years he went to his favourite public-house again, and wished for five pounds.

After he wished, a little man entered and spat the sovereigns into the tumbler, and they all drank all night.

59

Next morning Billy went back to his smithy. The devil, who had grown suspicious, turned himself into a sovereign and appeared on the floor. Billy seized the sovereign and clapped it into his purse. Then he took his purse and lay it upon the anvil, and began to beat it with his sledge-hammer, when the devil began to call out, "Spare my poor limbs, spare my poor limbs!"

"How much now if I let you go?" asked Billy

"Seven more years, three times the money, and one day in which to wish for what you like."

Billy took the sovereign out of his purse and threw it away, when he found his money in the smithy.

Billy carried on worse than ever; gambled and drank and raced, squandering it all before his seven years was gone. On the last day of his term he went to his favourite inn as usual and wished for a tumbler full of sovereigns. A little man with a big head, a big nose, and big mouth, a little body, and little legs, with clubbed feet and a forked tail, brought them in and put them in the tumbler. The drunkards in the room got scared when they saw the little man, for he looked all glowing with fire as he danced on the table. When he finished, he said, "Billy, to-morrow morning our compact is up."

"I know it, old boy, I know it, old boy!" said Billy. Then the devil ran out and disappeared, and the people began to question Billy:

"What is that? I think it is you, Mister Duffy, he is after."

"Oh, it is nothing at all," said Billy.

"I should think there was something," said the man.

"I am afraid my house will get a bad name," croaked the landlord.

"Not in the least! You are only a coward," said Billy.

"But in the name of God, what is it all about?" asked an old man.

"Oh, you'll see by-and-bye," said Billy; "it is nothing at all."

Next morning Billy went to his smithy, but the devil would not come near it.

So he went to his house, and began to quarrel with his wife, and whilst he was quarrelling the devil walked in and said:

"Well, Mr. Duffy, I am ready for you."

"Ah, yes; just sit down and wait a minute or two. I have some papers I want to put to rights before I go."

So the devil sat down in the arm-chair, and Billy went to the smithy and heated a pair of tongs red-hot, and coming back, he got the devil by the nose, and pulled it out as though it had been soft iron. And the devil began yelling, but he could not move, and Billy kept drawing the nose out till it was long enough to reach over the window, when he put an old bell-topper on the end of it. And the devil yelled, and snorted fire from his nose.

The whole of the village crowded round Billy's, house--at a safe distance--calling out, "Billy and the devil! The devil and Billy Duffy!"

The devil got awful savage, and blackguarded Billy Duffy terribly; but it was useless. Billy kept him there for days, till he got civil and said:

61

"Mr. Duffy, what will you let me go for?"

"Only one thing: I am to live the rest of my life without you, and have as much gold as I like."

The devil agreed, so Billy let him go; and immediately he grew rich. He lived to a good old age squandering money all the time, but at last he died and when he got to the gates of hell the clerk said "Who are you?" "Billy Duffy," said he. And when the devil, who was standing near, heard, he said:

"Good God! bar the gates and double-lock them for if this Billy Duffy the blacksmith gets in he will ruin us all."

Old Billy saw a pair of red-hot tongs, which he picked up, and seized the devil by the nose. When the devil pulled back his head he left a red-hot bit of his nose in the tongs.

Then Billy Duffy went up to the gates of heaven and St. Peter asked him who he was.

"Billy Duffy the blacksmith," he answered.

"No admittance! You are a bold, bad man," said St. Peter.

"Good God! what will I do?" said Billy, and he went back to the earth, where he and the piece of the devil's nose melted into a ball of fire, and he roves the earth till this day as a will-o'-the-wisp.

The Story of
John o' Groats

He was an old seaman, with weather-beaten face and black eyes, that had looked upon many lands and many sights.

"Well, indeed, I'll tell you about Johnny Groats as it was told to me one night in the trades," he said, blowing a whiff of smoke from his wheezy pipe.

"Well, in olden times there was a rich lord, who owned all the property looking on to the Pentlands--an awful place in bad weather; indeed, in any weather.

"He was a lone man, for his wife was dead, and his son had turned out to be a rake and a spendthrift, spending all his substance upon harlots and entertainments.

"Now this lord had a factor, by name John o' Scales, a stingy, cunning man, who robbed his master all he could during the week, and prayed hard for forgiveness on the Sabbath.

"The lord, who was getting very old, was much grieved on account of his son's behaviour. 'He'll spend everything when I am gone, and the estates will go into other hands,' the old man said to himself."

*   *   *   *   *

"One fine morning in summer the factor received orders to build a hut by the sea, and plant bushes and trees round about it. 'But

64

don't make the door to fit close; leave the space of a foot at the bottom, so the leaves can blow in, for I want the hut to shoot sea-fowl as they flight, and it is cold standing on the bare ground,' said the old man.

"The factor carried out his master's instructions, but not without suspicion of ulterior motives on his master's part. However, when he saw my lord shooting the birds and stuffing many of them his suspicions were allayed, and the factor thought that, after all, though his master wanted the hut for flight-shooting, still he must be getting softening of the brain, for it was very eccentric that he should take up this new hobby in his old age.

"So the old lord was never disturbed in his hut by curious and ill-timed visits.

"After a time the lord died, and was laid with his fathers, the prodigal inheriting the property.

"The old castle was then the scene of perpetual feastings and card parties, so that in a few years the property was heavily mortgaged, the old factor advancing the money.

"Things went apace, until one day the factor informed the young spendthrift that he had spent everything, and the estates were no longer his, so he gave him a few pounds, and turned him out.

"When the news spread round the countryside his old friends began to drop off, until at last the spendthrift found every door closed against him.

"When he had spent his last penny, the prodigal thought of the key which his father had given him, saying, 'When you have spent everything, take this key, and go to the hut.'

"But he had lost the key long before.

"Nevertheless, he went to the hut. It had a deserted appearance, being overgrown with moss and lichens.

"He managed to squeeze himself under the door, and when he stood up he saw a rope, with a noose hanging from the centre of the roof.
Pursuing his investigations, he found a parchment nailed to the back of the door, and in one corner stood an old three-legged stool. There was nothing else in the damp, mouldy room, so he began to read the parchment.

"'Thou art come to beggary; end thy miserable existence, for it is thy father's wish,' he read.

"He was dazed, and looked from the parchment to the rope, and from the rope to the parchment, saying to himself: 'Well, I have come to that, I must follow my father's wish.'

"So he got the stool and put it under the noose, and standing upon it, adjusted the rope with trembling fingers round his neck, when he said, hoarsely: 'Father, I do thy bidding,' and he kicked the stool from under him.

"Immediately he heard a crash, and found himself lying upon the leaves, with a feeling that his neck had been jerked off. However, he soon recovered, and, taking the noose from his neck, he looked up and saw an open trap-door in the ceiling. Placing the stool beneath the opening, he got on to it, and lifted himself through the trap-door, when he found himself in a loft, a parchment nailed to the wall facing him, and on the parchment was written, 'This has been prepared, for your end was foreseen, and your foolish father buried three chests of gold one foot below the surface of the floor of the hut. Go and take it and buy back your estate: marry, and beget an heir.'

"'Good God! is this a ghastly joke?' said the prodigal. But the words looked truthful; so he tore down the parchment, dropped through the trap-door, shut it, and readjusted the rope. He left the hut and borrowed a pick and shovel, and returning to the hut, he began to dig, and found one chest full of gold. When he made this discovery he closed the chest, filled in the hole, and spread leaves over the spot. He then ran off to his father's best friend, and told him of his good luck. They then called in two other friends, and consulted together how the old lord's wish was best to be carried out. 'I'll tell you,' said his father's oldest friend. 'Mr. John o' Scales gives a great dinner party once a month, and three of us here are invited as usual. You must come in, in the middle of dinner in your ordinary beggar clothes and beg humbly for some food, when he will give orders to have you turned out. Then you must begin to call him a liar and a thief, and accuse him of robbing your father and yourself of your inheritance. You'll see he'll get angry, and offer to let you have it back.'

"So the prodigal dug up the chests, and carted the money away in canvas bags, storing it at his friend's house."

*   *   *   *   *

"When the night of the dinner party came, the prodigal drove up to the castle in a cart filled with canvas bags. Jumping off his seat by the driver, he went into the feast in his beggar's clothes, and going up to the host, he begged humbly for some food.

"'Go from this house! What business have you here?' asked the host.

"Most of the gentlemen and ladies began to frown upon him, and murmur against him, as he walked to the lady of the house and begged her to give him some food, but she replied:

"'Oh, thou spendthrift! thou fool of fools! if all fools were hanged, as they ought to be, you'd be the first.'

"Then the beggar's countenance changed, a deep flush of anger overspread his features, and drawing himself up to his full height, he said, with solemn voice, addressing the host:

"'Thou hast robbed my father all the days of his life, and thou hast robbed the orphan. May the curse of God be upon you!'

"The host grew furious; then he looked ashamed, and shouted angrily:

"'Bring me £40,000, and you shall have your estate back. I never robbed you, but you lost your inheritance by your own follies.'

"'Gentlemen,' said the beggar, 'I take you all to witness that this thief says I can have my estate back for L40,000.'

"The people murmured, and the three friends said: 'We are witnesses.'

"The beggar ran out into the night, and returned with a man laden with sacks, and they began to count out £40,000 upon a side-table, where a haunch of venison still smoked.

"When they had counted out the money, the beggar said:

"'There is your £40,000; sign this receipt.'

"The amazed factor drew back, when the three friends said:

"'You must sign; you are a gentleman of your word, of course.'

"Mechanically John o' Scales signed the paper.

"'And now,' said the former beggar, 'leave my house at once, with your wife--you coward! you cur! You robbed my father, and then cheated me when I was a spendthrift. Begone, and may your name be accursed in the land!'

"And the son turned all out except his three friends.

"In a few months he married the daughter of one of his friends; but he never gambled again, only entertaining his three friends and their families, who came and went as they liked.

"And from that day John o' Scales was called John o' Groats."

Eva's Buck

As black-eyed, black-haired Eva Sauvet was walking one day in Jersey she saw a lozenge-marked snake, whereupon she ran away frightened.

When she got home and told her mother, the old woman said:

"Well, child, next time you see the snake give it your handkerchief."

The next day Eva went out with beating heart, and ere long she saw the snake come gliding out from the bushes, so she threw down her handkerchief, for she was too frightened to hand it to the snake.

The snake's eyes gleamed and twinkled, and taking the handkerchief into his fangs, he made off to an old ruin, whither Eva followed.

But when they got to the ruin the snake disappeared, and Eva ran home to tell her mother.

Next day, Pere Sauvet and some men went to the ruin, where Eva showed the hole where the snake had disappeared.

Old Pere Sauvet lit a fire, and smoked the snake out, killing it with a stick as it glided over the stones.

After that they dug out the hole, when they found the handkerchief. Digging still further along, they came upon a hollow place, at the bottom of which they found a lot of gold.

The Fishermen of Shetland

There was a snug little cove in one of the Shetland Islands. At the head of the cove stood a fishing hamlet, containing some twenty huts. In these huts lived the fisher-folk, ruled by one man—the chief - who was the father of two beautiful daughters.

Now these fishermen for some years had been very lucky, for a fairy queen and her fairies had settled there, and she had given her power over to a merman, who was the chief of a large family of mermaids. The fairy queen had made the merman a belt of sea-weed, which he always wore round his body. The merman used to turn the water red, green, and white, at noon each day, so that the fishermen knew that if they cast their nets into the coloured waters they would make good hauls.

Amongst these fishermen were two brave brothers, who courted the chief's daughters, but the old man would not let them get married until they became rich men.

Whenever the fishermen went off in the boats the merman was used to sit on a rock, and watch them fishing.

Close by the hamlet was a great wood, in which lived a wicked old witch and a dwarf.

Now this witch wished to get possession of the merman's belt, and so gain the fairy's power. Telling her scheme to the dwarf, she said to him:

"Now you must trap the merman when he is sitting on the rocks

72

watching the fishing fleet. But I must change you into a bee, when you must suck of the juice in this magic basin, then fly off and alight on the merman's head, when he will fall asleep."

So the dwarf agreed, and it happened as she had said; and the merman fell asleep, and the dwarf stole the belt and brought it to the witch.

"Now you must wear the belt," said the witch to the dwarf, "and you will have the power and the fairy will lose her power."

They then translated the sleeping merman to the forest and laid him before the hut, when the witch got a copper vessel, saying:

"We must bury him in this."

Then she got the magic pot, and told the dwarf to take a ladleful of the fluid in the pot, and pour it over the merman, which he did, and immediately the merman turned into smoke, that settled in the copper vessel. Then they sealed the copper vessel tightly.

"Now take this vessel, and heave it into the sea fifty miles from the land," said the witch, and the dwarf did as he was bid.

"Now we'll starve those old fishermen out this winter," said the witch; and it happened as she had said--they could catch nothing.

In the spring the queen fairy came to one of the young fishermen who was courting one of the chief's daughters, and said:

"You must venture for the sake of your love, and for the lives of the fishermen, or you will all starve--but I will be with you. Will you run the risk?"

"I will," said the brave fisherman.

"Well, the dwarf has got my belt, he stole it from the merman, and so I have lost power over the world for twelve months and a day; but if you get back the belt I can settle the witch; if not, you will all starve and catch no fish."

So the bold fisherman agreed to try.

"Now I must transform you into a bear, and you'll have to watch the witch and the dwarf, and take your chance of getting the belt; and you must watch where he hides his treasure, for he is using the belt as a means to get gold, which he hides in a cave."

And so the sailor was turned into a bear, and he went to the wood and watched the dwarf, and saw that he hid his treasure in a cave in some crags.

The bear had been given the power of making himself invisible, by sitting on his haunches and rubbing his ears with his paws.

One night, when it was very boisterous, the bear felt like going to see his sweetheart. So he went, and knocked at the door. The girl opened the door, and shrieked when she saw the bear.

"Oh, let him in," said her old mother.

So the bear came in and asked for shelter from the storm, for he could speak.

And he went and sat by the fire, and asked his sweetheart to brush the snow from his coat, which she did.

"I won't do you any harm," he said; "let me sleep by the fire."

He came again the next night, and they gave him some gruel, and played with him; for he was just like a dog.

So he came every night until the springtime, when, one morning, as he was going away, he said:

"You mustn't expect me any more. Spring has come, and the snows have melted. I can't come again till the summer is over."

So he returned to the wood and watched the dwarf, but he could never catch him without his belt, until one day he saw him fishing for salmon without the belt, and at the same time his sweetheart and her sister came by picking flowers.

So the bear went up to the dwarf, and the dwarf, when he saw him coming, said:

"Ah! good bear! good bear! let me go. These two girls will be a more dainty morsel for you."

But the bear smote him with his paw and killed him, and immediately the bear was turned into his former self, and the girls ran up and kissed him, and talked.

Then he took the two girls to the dwarf's cave, and gave each of them a bag of treasure, keeping one for himself. And taking the belt, he put it on, and they all walked back to the hamlet, when he told the fishermen that their troubles would soon be over-- but that he must kill the witch first.

Then he turned the belt three times, and said:

"I wish for the queen fairy."

And she came, and was delighted, and said: "Now you must come and slay the witch," and she handed him a bow and arrow, telling him to use it right and tight when he got to the hut.

So he went off to the wood, and found the witch in her hut, and she begged for mercy.

"Oh no, you have done too much mischief," he said, and he shot her.

Then the queen fairy appeared, and sent him to gather dry wood to make a fire. When the fire was made she sent him to fetch the witch's wand, which she cast into the flames, saying:

"Now, mark my word, all the devils of hell will be here."

And when the wand began to burn all the devils came and tried to snatch it from the fire, but the queen raised her wand, saying:

> "Through this powerful wand
> that I hold in my hand,
> Through this bow and arrow
> I have caused her to be slain,
> That she may leave our domain.
> Now take her up high
> into the sky,
> And let her burst asunder
> as a clap of thunder.
> Then take her to hell
> and there let her dwell,
> To all eternity."

And the wand was burnt, and the devils carried the witch off in a noise like thunder.

The twelve months were up on that day, and the fairy said to the fisherman:

"Take your chief and your brother, and put out to sea half-a-mile, where you'll see a red spot, bright as the sun on the water; cast in your net on the sea-side of the spot, and pull to the shore."

They did as the queen commanded, and when they pulled the net on the shore they found the copper vessel.

"Now open it," said the queen to the fisherman with the belt, "but cover your belt with your coat first."

And he did so, and when he opened the copper a ball of smoke rose into the air, and suddenly the merman stood before them, and said:

> "The first four months that I was in prison,
>   I swore I'd make the man as rich as a king,
>   The man who released me.
>   But there was no release, no release, no release.
>
>   The second four months that I was in prison,
>   I swore I'd make the water run red,
>   But there was no release, no release, no release.
>
>   The last four months that I was in prison,
>   I swore in my wrath I'd take my deliverer's life,
>   Whoever he might be."

Whereupon the fisherman opened his coat and showed him the belt. Then the merman immediately cooled down, and said:

"Oh, that's how I came into this trouble."

Then he asked the fisherman with the belt what had happened, and he told him the whole story.

Then the queen told the fisherman to take the girdle off and put it back on the merman, and he did so; and suddenly the merman took to the sea, and began to sing from a rock:

> "As I sit upon the rock,
> I am like a statue block,
> And I straighten my hair,
> That is so long and fair.
> And now my eyes look bright,
> For I am in great delight,
> Because I am free in glee,
> To roam over the sea."

After that the hamlet was joyful again, for the fishermen began to catch plenty of fish; for the merman showed them where to cast their nets, by colouring the water as of old.

And the two brothers married the chief's two beautiful daughters, and they lived happily ever afterwards.

The Pastor's Nurse

Mon pere etait tres jeune encore quand il est entre au saint ministere et qu'il fut nomme pasteur a Hambach, village de la Lorraine. L'endroit etait assez grand, mais de peu de ressources, et il etait heureux de trouver quelqu'un qui, dans son inexperience et loin de sa famille, fut capable de lui aider a fonder sa maison, selon les usages et les traditions d'un bon presbytere.

C'est Madame Catherine Reeb, personne d'un age mur, dont le mari avait ete instituteur, mais qui d'une nature mecontente et orgueilleuse, se croyait au-dessus de sa sphere, et faisait sentir a sa pauvre femme, qui l'aimait d'un devouement admirable, toutes les tortures que l'egoisme peut inventer. Elle se donna a peine le necessaire pour procurer a son seigneur et maitre tous les soins que sa superiorite imaginaire pouvait exiger, et pourtant il ne fut jamais content, et un beau jour disparut, sans qu'on put retrouver ses traces. La pauvre Catherine fut inconsolable, mais ne perdit pas l'espoir qu'un jour son mari ne revint, charge de tous les honneurs, qu'elle aussi, bonne ame credule, lui croyait dus.

C'est dans ces conditions qu'elle vint tenir le menage de mon pere, elle le fit avec beaucoup de tact et de douceur, mais tout en elle respirait la tristesse, l'abandon. Quand, apres quelques annees, mon pere se maria, Catherine continua son activite dans la maison, mais avec son bon sens naturel, en refera la responsabilite a sa jeune maitresse, qu'elle aimait beaucoup.

Ma mere chercha par bien des moyens a la distraire de son chagrin. Elle devint plus gaie, quand elle nous raconta des histoires et fit des jeux avec nous. Nos parents se faisaient un plaisir de l'observer parfois quand elle ne s'endouta pas, se disant: "Voila ce qu'il fallait a notre vieille Catherine, ce sont les enfants qui lui ont porte l'oubli."

Mais cela ne devait pas durer bien longtemps. Elle redevint peu a peu silencieuse, et ses profonds soupirs ne prouverent que trop que l'oubli du triste passe n'etait qu'a la surface; ses manieres taciturnes et les manifestations d'une secrete inquietude commencaient meme a troubler mes parents, et mon pere essaya par beaucoup de bonte a la persuader d'accepter les epreuves de sa vie comme venant de Dieu. Elle pleura beaucoup et s'efforca de se gagner un peu de calme, mais sans fruit.

Un beau jour elle vint trouver mon pere et lui dit: "Mon cher maitre, aidez-moi a executer mon projet, et surtout n'essayez pas de m'en dissuader. Je suis decidee a aller a la recherche de mon mari; je sais qu'il a besoin de moi, il m'appelle, et je vais partir. Procurez-moi les papiers et certificats necessaires a cette entreprise, afin que je ne sois pas inquietee par le police. J'irai ou mes pieds me conduiront, je ne sais ou je le retrouverai, mais je sais que je le reverrai. Je marcherai de jour, et de nuit je me logerai dans une auberge ou une ferme, et je vous donnerai de mes nouvelles."

Mon pere voyait qu'il ne pouvait ebranler sa resolution, fit ce qu'elle lui demanda, pourvoyant tant que possible aux besoins de la route, et c'est le coeur gros de sinistres presages que mes parents virent partir leur bonne et fidele servante. Quand je lui dis: "Tu ne nous aimes donc plus, puisque tu pars?" elle m'embrassa en pleurant, et dit, "Je reviendrai!" Il y avait alors vingt ans depuis la disparition de son mari, pendant lesquel elle avait soigneusement entretenu son menage dans une petite maison qui lui, appartenait.

Elle partit donc, ainsi qu'elle l'avait dit; marchant de jour et se reposant de nuit, se dirigeant vers la Prusse.

Elle fut absente sans que nous eussions de ses nouvelles pendant au-dela d'un mois quand un jour le facteur apporte une lettre a mon pere de la part d'un collegue inconnu d'un village de la Prusse, qui lui dit: "Une femme de respectable apparence, munie de certificates identifiant ses dires, est venue me prier de proceder a l'humation de son mari qu'elle a trouve mort dans un bois du village voisin. L'autorite municipale a compare les papiers trouves dans les poches de l'inconnu et a constate qu'ils sont en rapport avec ceux que la femme Reeb porte sur elle, et sur ce fait, et voyant que l'homme etait mort sans violence, a laisse ses restes a elle qui se dit sa veuve et qui lui a rendu les derniers honneurs au cimetiere de notre village."

Inutile de decrire la surprise de mes parents a la reception de cette lettre, qui fut bientot suivie par le retour de Catherine. Elle completa le recit du pasteur en disant qu'un matin en sortant de ce village, elle alla trouver un petit bois, quand elle vit au bord du chemin un homme etendu mort, mais qui venait seulement de cesser de vivre. Elle le regarda, l'examina et reconnut son mari; il lui parut evident qu'il faisait son retour vers la patrie et elle, mais que la mort l'avait surpris en route. Catherine fut bien plus calme apres ces evenements, mais ses forces declinerent et dans la meme annee on creusa pour elle une tombe au cimetiere de Hambach. Elle n'avait plus de famille que celle qu'elle avait si fidelement servie, et les larmes de deux jeunes enfants prouverent que quoique abandonnee elle avait ete aimee.

otes

(1) THE FAIRIES OF CARAGONAN.
Source: This story came from a Welsh pedlar--a woman. Its genuineness may be relied upon. I find it a common belief that fairies have power over witches, and the witch-hare is commonly believed in; also a witch-fox. I have heard of no evil fairies in Wales; all the mischief seems to be the work of witches. I have
heard several variants of the witch-hare.

(2) THE CRAIG-Y-DON BLACKSMITH.
This story I have heard from four different persons.

(3) OLD GWILYM.
Source: This story came from an old Welshman who says he knew Gwilym, and heard the story from his lips. The narrator may be relied upon.

(4) THE BABY-FARMER.
Same source.

(5) THE OLD MAN AND THE FAIRIES.
Same source as 2. In Wales, so far as I have heard, the disappointed always find _cockle-shells_.

(6) TOMMY PRITCHARD.
Same source as 2.

(7) KADDY'S LUCK.
Same source as 2.

(8) STORY OF GELERT.
As told by an old fisherman. The variant of this well-known story may prove useful. Borrow's "tent" theory is, I think, an invention of his own. I was fortunate enough to get possession of an old book (without title-page, title, or author's name), in which the following remarks on this story occur:--

"Some say this should be written Bedd Gelert, or Gilert, signifying Gelert's, or Gilert's Grave. To this name is annexed a traditional story, which it is hardly worth while to mention. However, the substance of the tradition is, that Prince Llewelyn ap Iorwerth, in a fit of passion, killed a favourite greyhound in this place, named Gelert, or Gilert, and that, repenting of the deed, he caused a tomb to be erected over his grave, where afterwards the parish church was built. See the story at large in Mr. Edw. Jones's "Welsh Music". But we may reasonably conclude that this is all a fable, both when we consider the impiety of building a church for divine worship over the grave of a dog, an impiety not consistent with the genius of that age; and when we consider, also, that the establishment of parochial cures, and the building of our country churches in Wales, began soon after the dispersion of the British clergy, which happened at the time of the massacre at Bangor Iscoed, A.D. 603, at the instigation of Augustine the Monk, employed for that purpose by the See of Rome. Llewelyn ap Iorwerth governed Wales from A.D. 1194 to 1240, when he died; so that parish churches were built between five and six hundred years before the time of this prince.

"This Gelert, or Gilert, must, in all probability, have been some old monk or saint of that name, who was interred here, and was either the first founder of this church, or one to whose memory it was dedicated, if built after his time. Bethgelert, before the Reformation, was a priory. Lewis Dwnn, a bard of the fifteenth century, in a poem (the purport of which is to solicit David, the Prior of Bethgelert, to bestow on John Wynne, of Gwydwr, Esq., a fine bay horse which he possessed) extols the Prior for his liberality and learning. Hence we are led to suppose that this monk was very opulent, and a popular character in his time."

The stories of a hunter killing his favourite greyhound (always a greyhound) are common to many districts. The book quoted is said to be written by a Mr. Williams, in 1800.

(9) ORIGIN OF THE WELSH.
Source: An old seaman, who avers he heard it on a ship, on the way home from Calcutta. I look with suspicion on the story. However, the Welsh always believed they were descended from the Trojans, and the author of the book cited says on this point:--

"Elen was a very common name among the ancient British ladies, and it seems to have been often bestowed out of compliment upon genteel and beautiful women; as we sometimes hear at this day "Ei Elen O" (his Elen) when a man has a young and beautiful wife; and there is hardly a love-song but the woman is called or compared in it to the Trojan Helena, or Elen, as the Welsh write and pronounce the word.
The Welsh have had amongst them, time out of mind, a tradition that the first colony of Bretons came to these islands from Troy after the destruction of that city."

(10) THE STORY OF THE CROWS.
Source: Told me by an old man, who knew the defunct.

(11) ROBERTS AND THE FAIRIES.
Source: Told me by another old man, and I believe it to be genuine.
There is another story of the same kind, of a man who was searching for treasure in Beaumaris Castle, and after he had told of his luck a stone fell on him, so that he had to go away.

(12) THE QUEEN OF THE DELL.
Came from the same old pedlar as No. 1. A genuine story. The narrator says you seldom hear a fairy story in Anglesea unless there is a witch in it.

(13) ELLEN'S LUCK.
Source: Told me by the same old man as No. 11. I believe it to be genuine, and the narrator trustworthy.

(14) THE PELLINGS.
Source: Taken _verbatim_ from the old book referred to. In the context the author says these people inhabited the districts about the foot of Snowdon, and were known by the nickname of Pellings, which is not yet extinct; and he says they tell the tale as given.
After telling the story, which he entitles a fairy story, he makes the following suggestive comments:--
"Before the Reformation, when the Christian world was enveloped in Popish darkness and superstition, when the existence of fairies and other spectres was not questioned, and when such a swarm of idle people, under the names of minstrels, poets, begging friars, etc., were permitted to ramble about, it may be supposed that these vagrants had amongst themselves some kind of rule or government, if I may so term it, as we are assured those that now-a-days go under the name of gypsies have. Such people might, at appointed times on

fine moonlight nights, assemble in some sequestered spot, to regulate their dark affairs and divide the spoil; and then perform their nightly _orgies_, so as to terrify people from coming near them, lest their tricks and cheats should be discovered. It is possible the men of Ystrad might have less superstition, and somewhat more courage, than their neighbours, and supposing such a one to come suddenly on these nightly revellers, he would of course cause great consternation amongst them; and, on finding a comely female in the group, it is not unnatural to imagine that he might, as the heroes of old have done before him, seize on a beauteous Helen, carry her home, and in process of time marry her--for many valorous knights have done the latter; but she, on account of some domestic jars, might afterwards have eloped from him, and returned to her former companions and occupation."

The author makes the following remarks in a foot-note:--

"The English writers of romances feign the fairies to be of a smaller size than even the fabled pigmies; the Welsh people ever supposed them to be of the same stature with mankind. Shakespeare describes his fairy as less than a mite, riding through people's brains to make the chase. This has not been my experience. I have had them described to me of all sizes, varying from a woman to little people two feet high. They have been described, when large, as dressed like ordinary ladies, when small, with short dresses; no hats, and hair in a plaited pigtail down the back."

Finally, the writer says:

"What other interpretation can be given to this tale I know not. This, and such other tales, the material of which one might collect a volume, must, it may reasonably be supposed, have something of reality for their origin and foundation, before they were dressed out in the familiar garb given them by their authors."

So our author is a "realist" as regards the origin of fairies.

(15) THE LONG-LIVED ANCESTORS.
Source: Taken _verbatim_ from the book quoted. This fable refers to the place, _Cwm Caw Lwyd_, regarding which the writer says:

"With regard to the _Cwm Caw Lwyd_, there is a still extant fable entitled _Creaduriaid Hir Hoedlog_ (i.e., the long-lived ancestors), which seems to be a composition of no modern date. At present the moral of it cannot be elucidated; but it seems that, in one respect, it was intended to represent the solitariness of this place, inhabited only by the weeping owl from remote antiquity; and certainly it is the most solitary and romantic retreat that the mind of man could imagine." The writer says his is a "literal translation of the story, according to the Welsh phraseology".

(16) THE GIANTESS'S APRON-FULL.
Source: [Verbatim] from the same book. Referring to the heaps of stone found on the hill-tops, he gives the fable of the heap found upon _Bwlchy Ddeufaen_, which he says is called _Ban Clodidd y Gawres_--literally, the giantess's apron-full.

"The writer regards such tales as originally intended as hyperboles, to magnify the prowess and magnanimity of renowned persons."

(17) A FABLE.

Source: Taken _verbatim_ from the same book. The writer quotes it apropos of the Roman custom of bribing the Britons on the mountain tops. We are told the fable was delivered by one of the Britons, named _Gwrgan Farfdrwch_, who spoke to this effect, and then follows the fable.

(18) THE STORY OF THE PIG-TROUGH.
Source: Told by Hugh's daughter. Genuine.

(19) BILLY DUFFY AND THE DEVIL.
Source: Told me by the old man who told me of the origin of the Welsh. Vague.

(20) JOHN O' GROATS.
Same source. Vague.

(21) EVA'S LUCK.
Source: A Jersey fisherman. Reliable. He also informed me that large stones, supported on others, were called "Fairy Stones" in Jersey.

(22) THE FISHERMEN OF SHETLAND.

Source: Told me by a yachting hand, who heard it from a Shetlander named Abernethy who was serving in the same yacht with him. Not many years ago, some volunteers at Beaumaris swore they saw a mermaid there, and fired several shots at it. I think this story to be genuine and beautiful.

(23) THE PASTOR'S NURSE.
Source: Reliable. Written for me by the Pastor's mother in
French. Given verbatim,

FINAL.

The book I have quoted is in my possession, and was written, I
am told, by a Mr. Williams, a Welshman, of Llandegai in
Anglesea. That he was shrewd, reasonable, and knew the people
of North Wales thoroughly, is evident from the context. The
book has no date, but appears to have been written in 1800.

Lightning Source UK Ltd.
Milton Keynes UK
UKOW042236040313

207128UK00001B/4/P